Music Notebook

CHECK OUT ALL OUR UNIQUE NOTEBOOKS ON AMAZON

nameworkspress@gmail.com

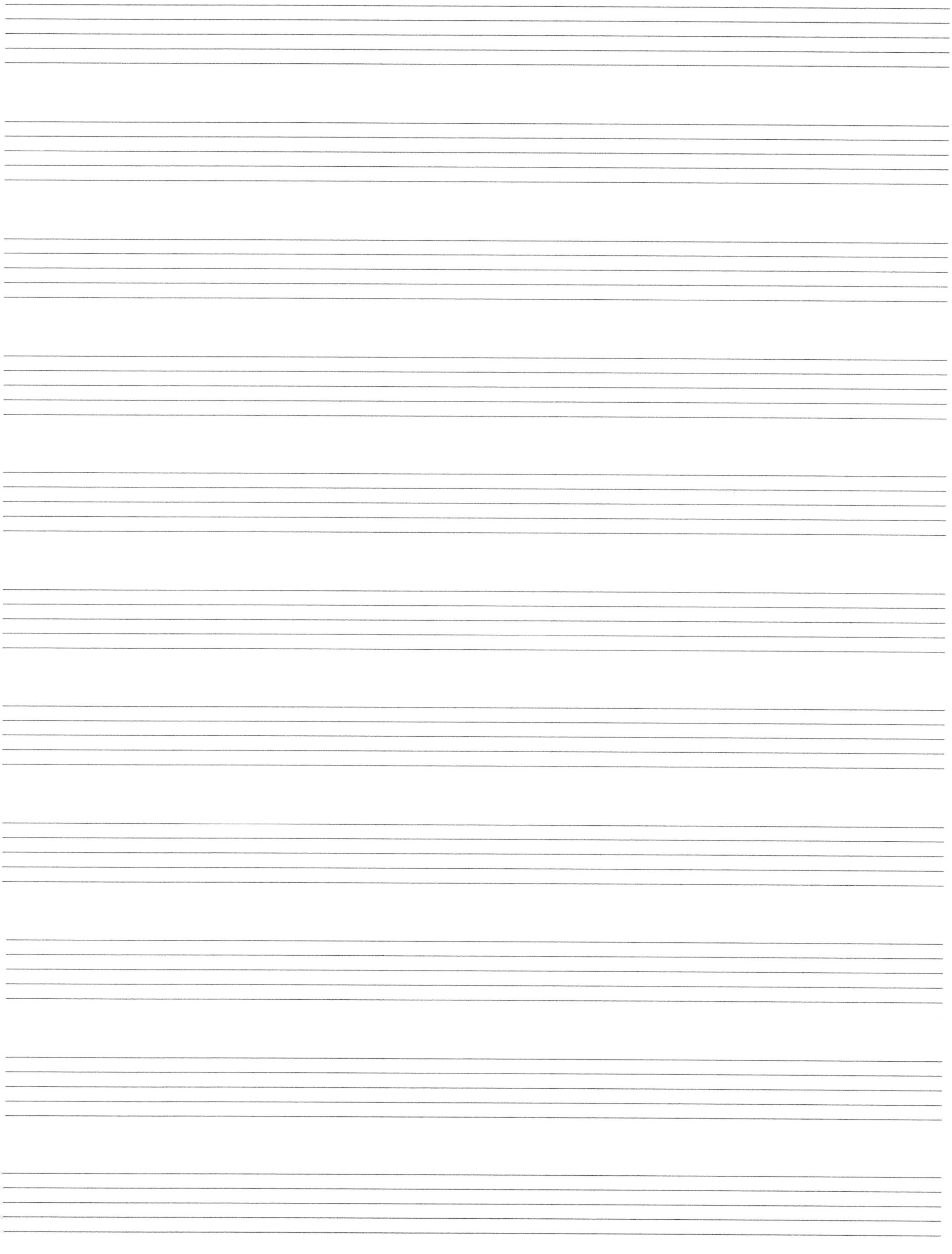

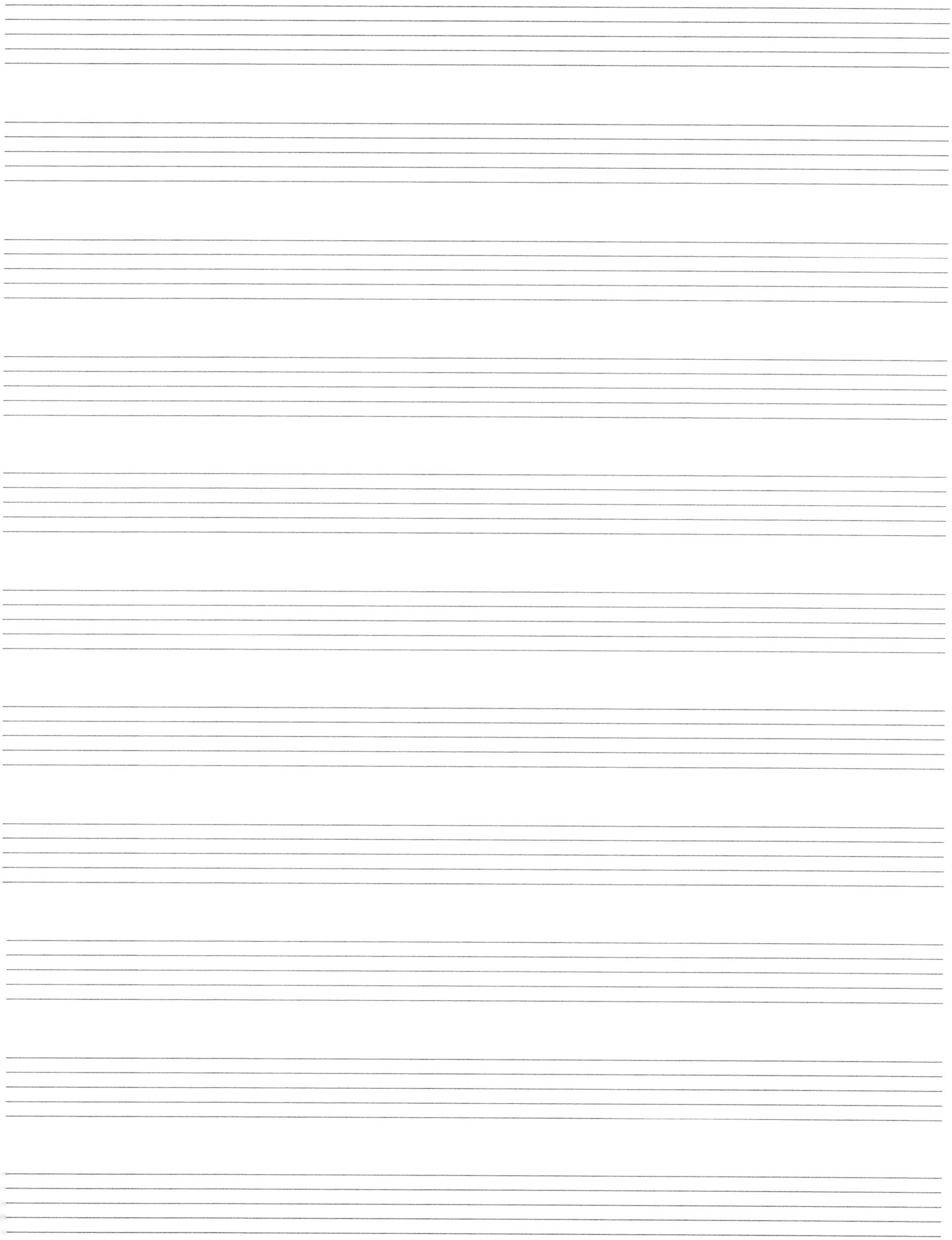

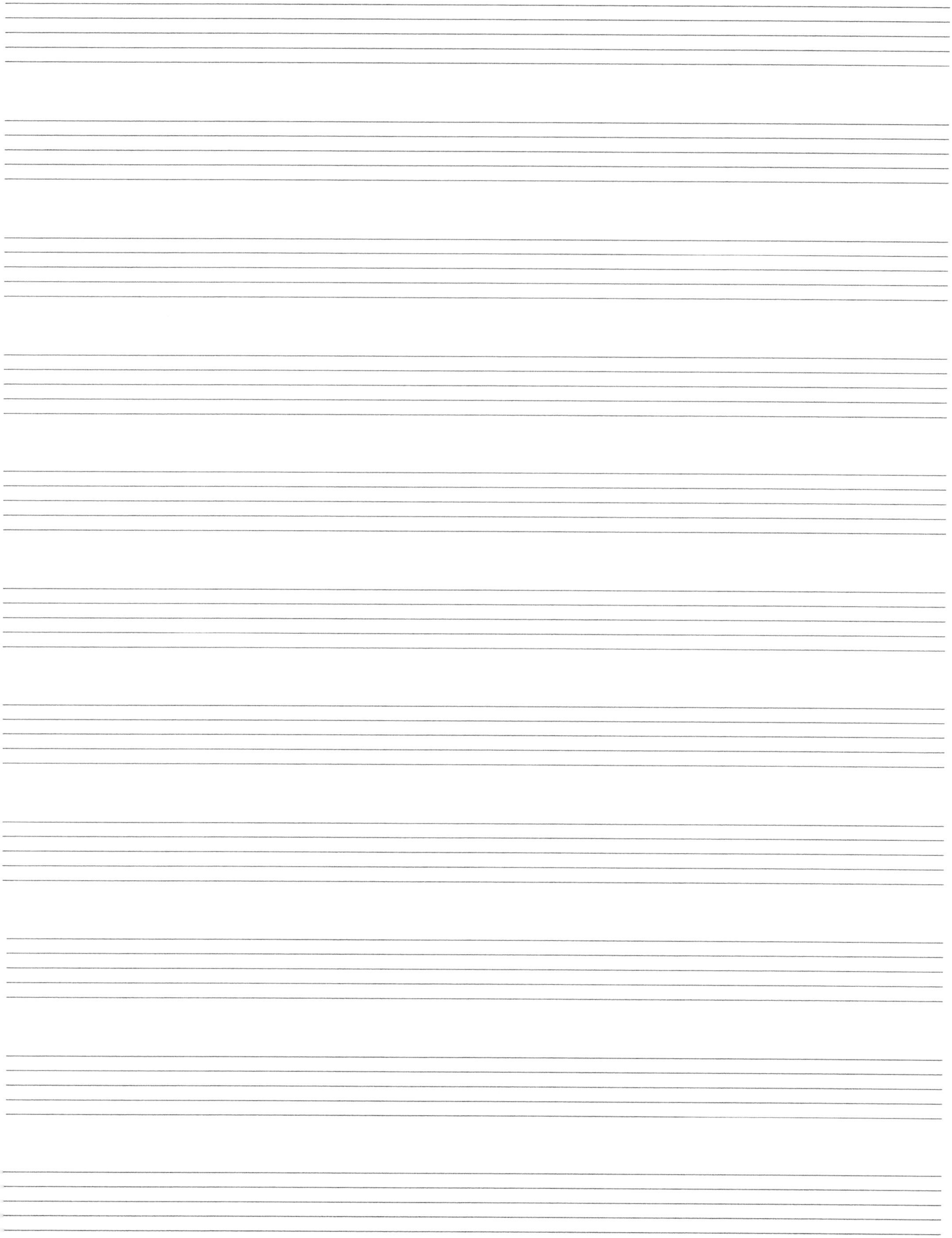

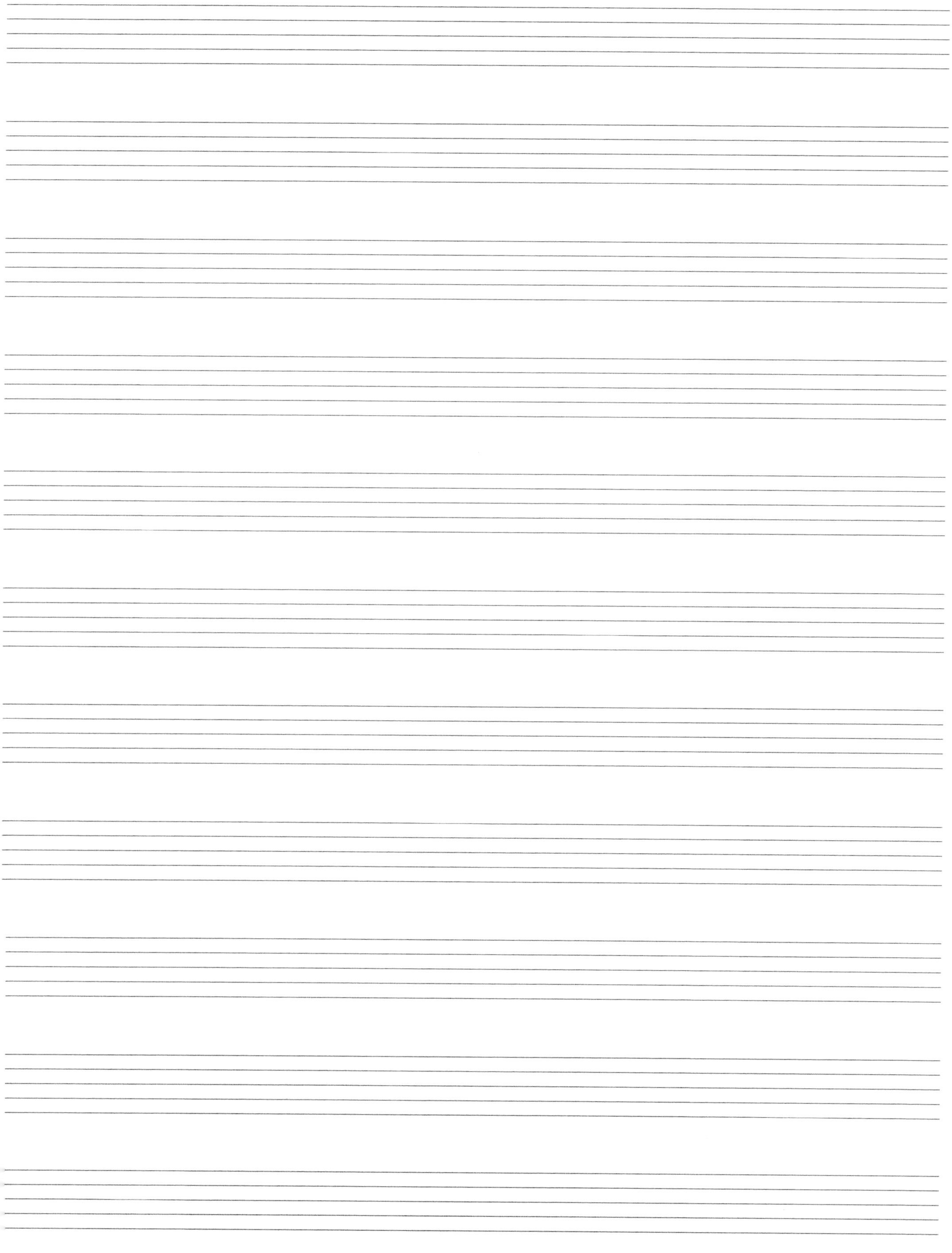

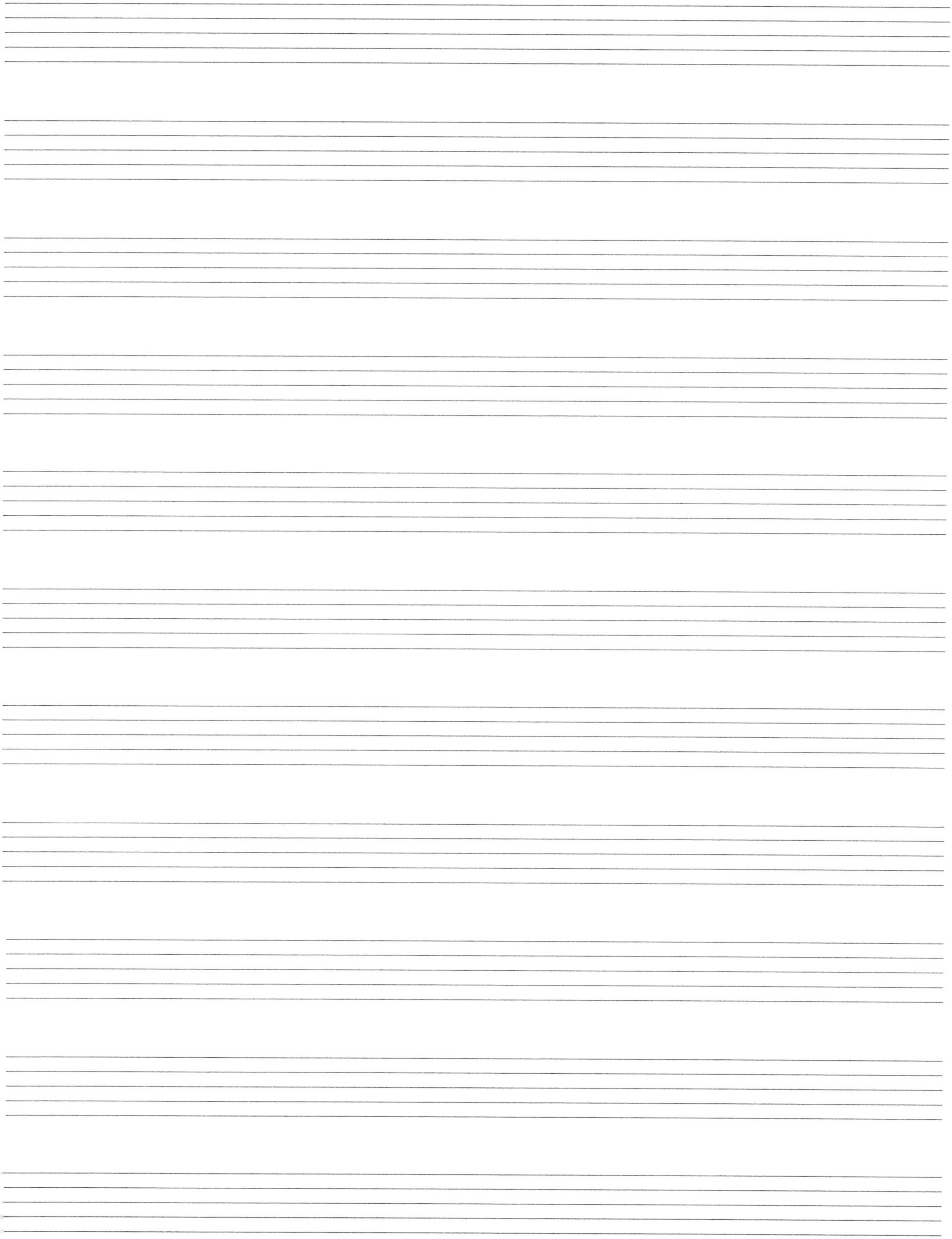

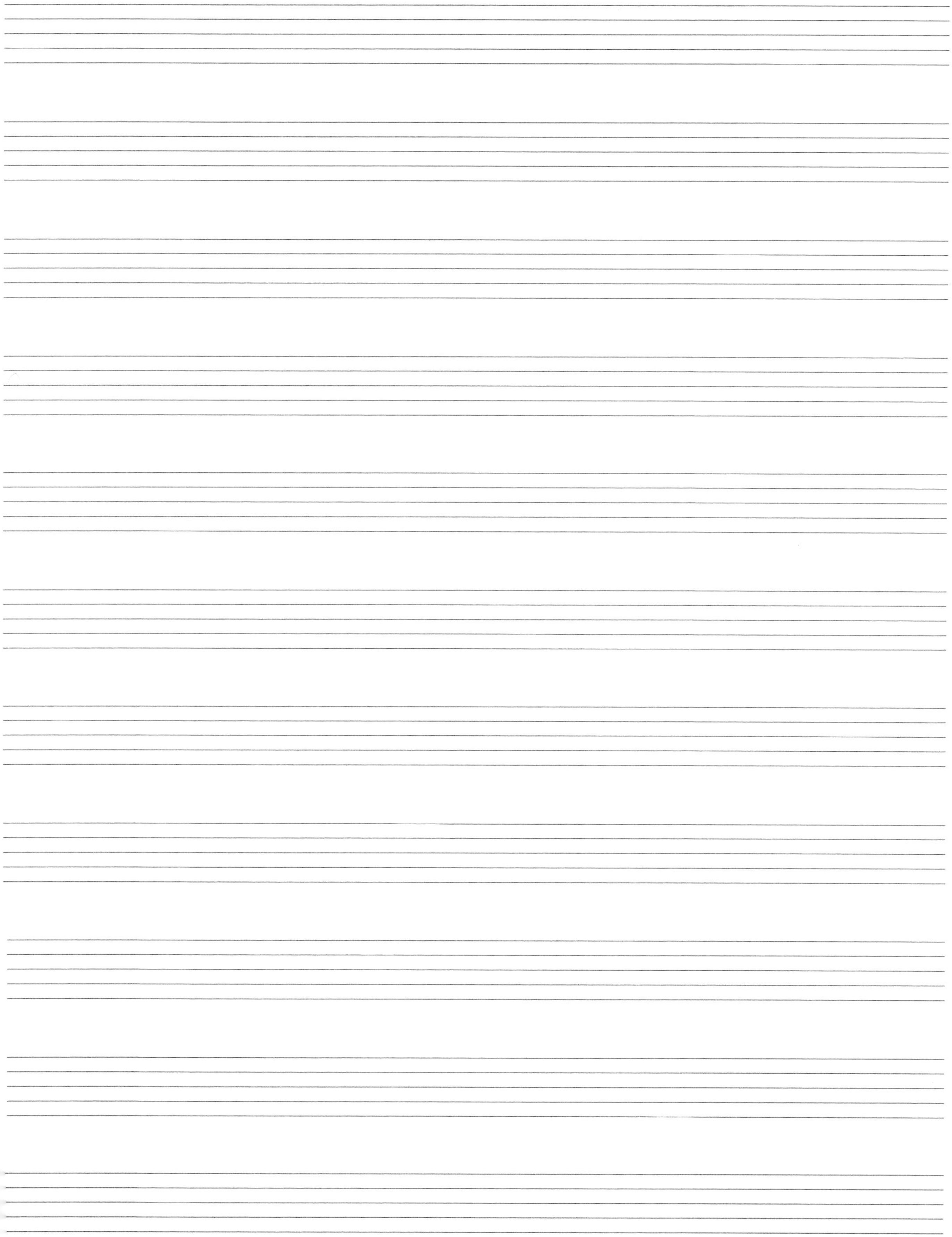

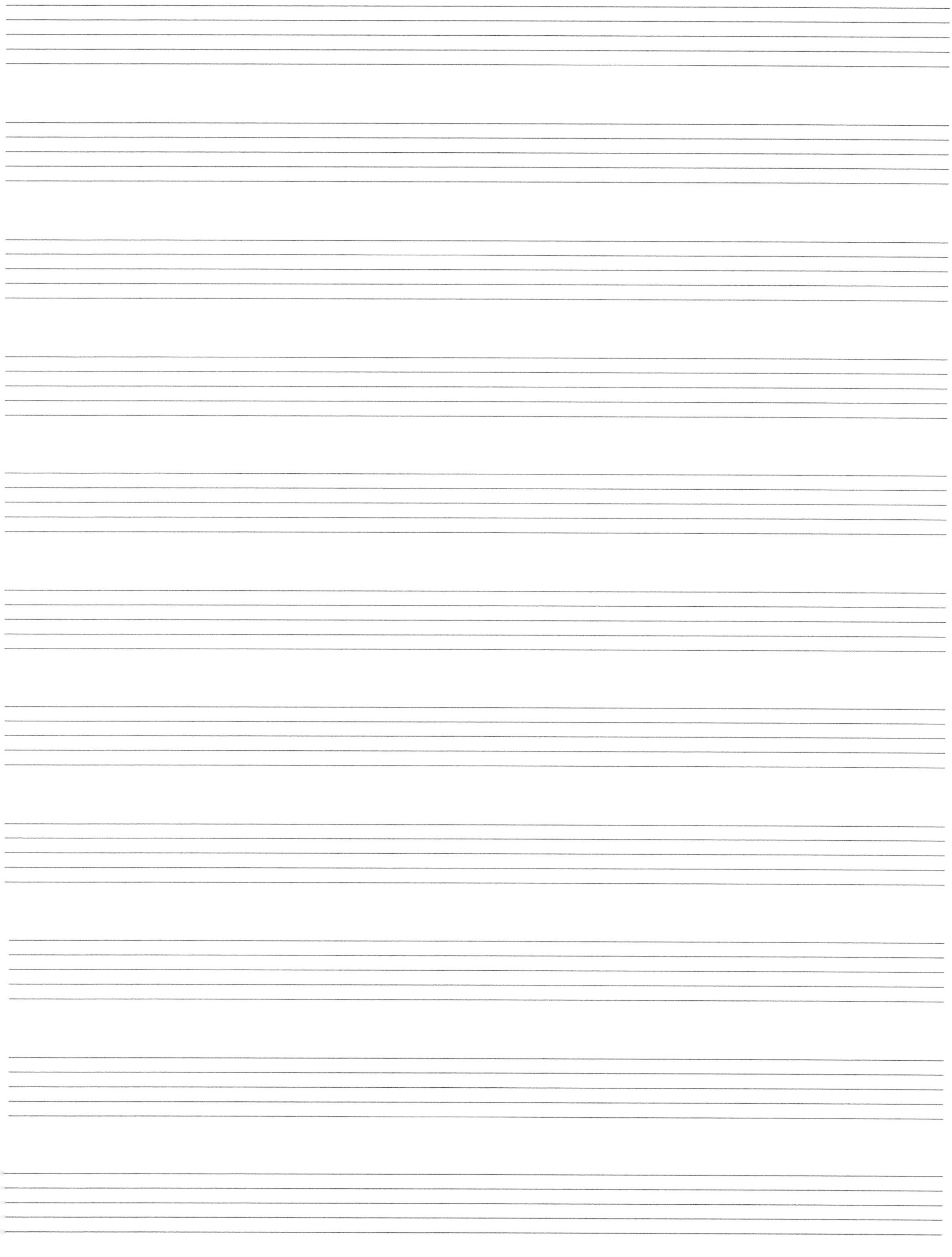

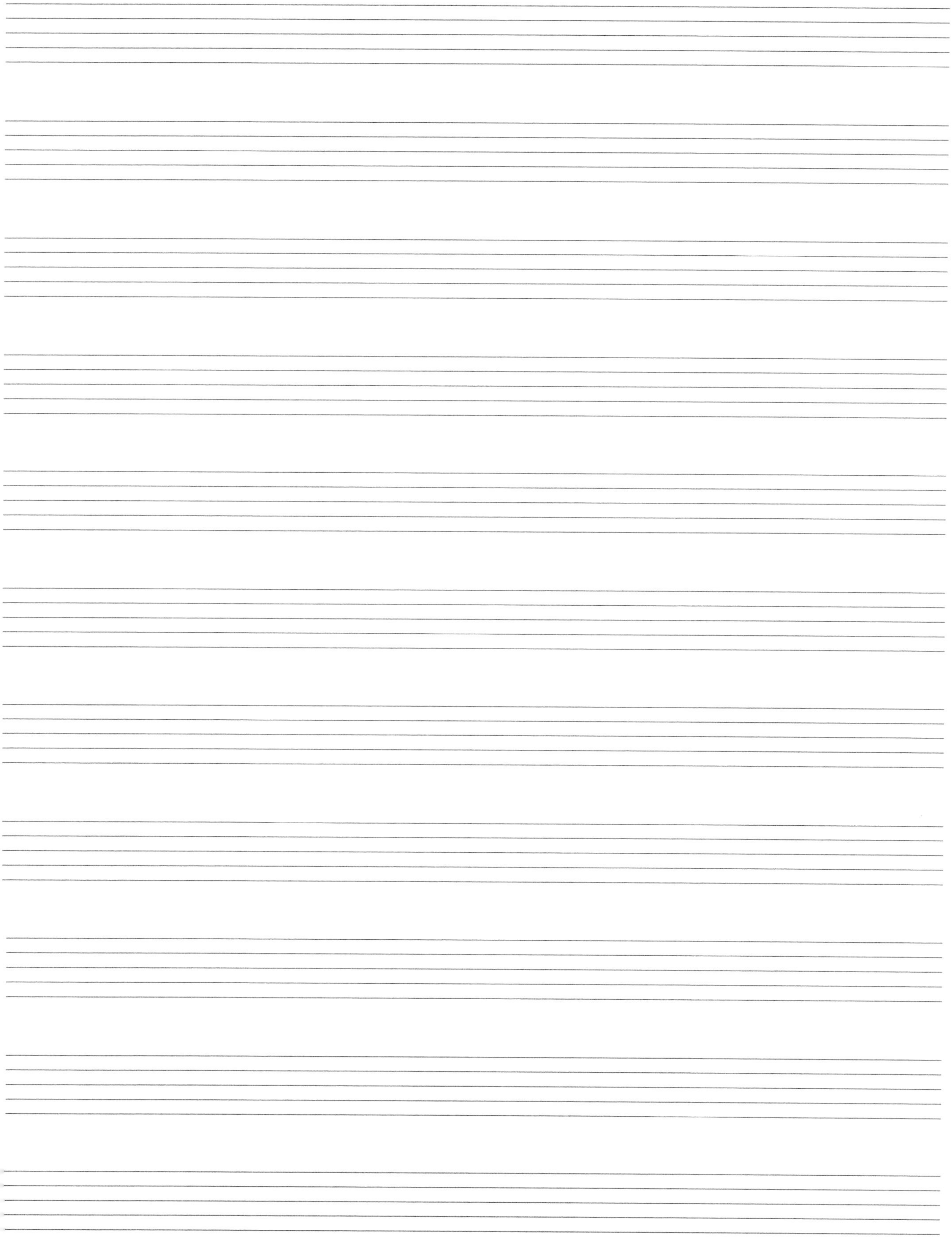

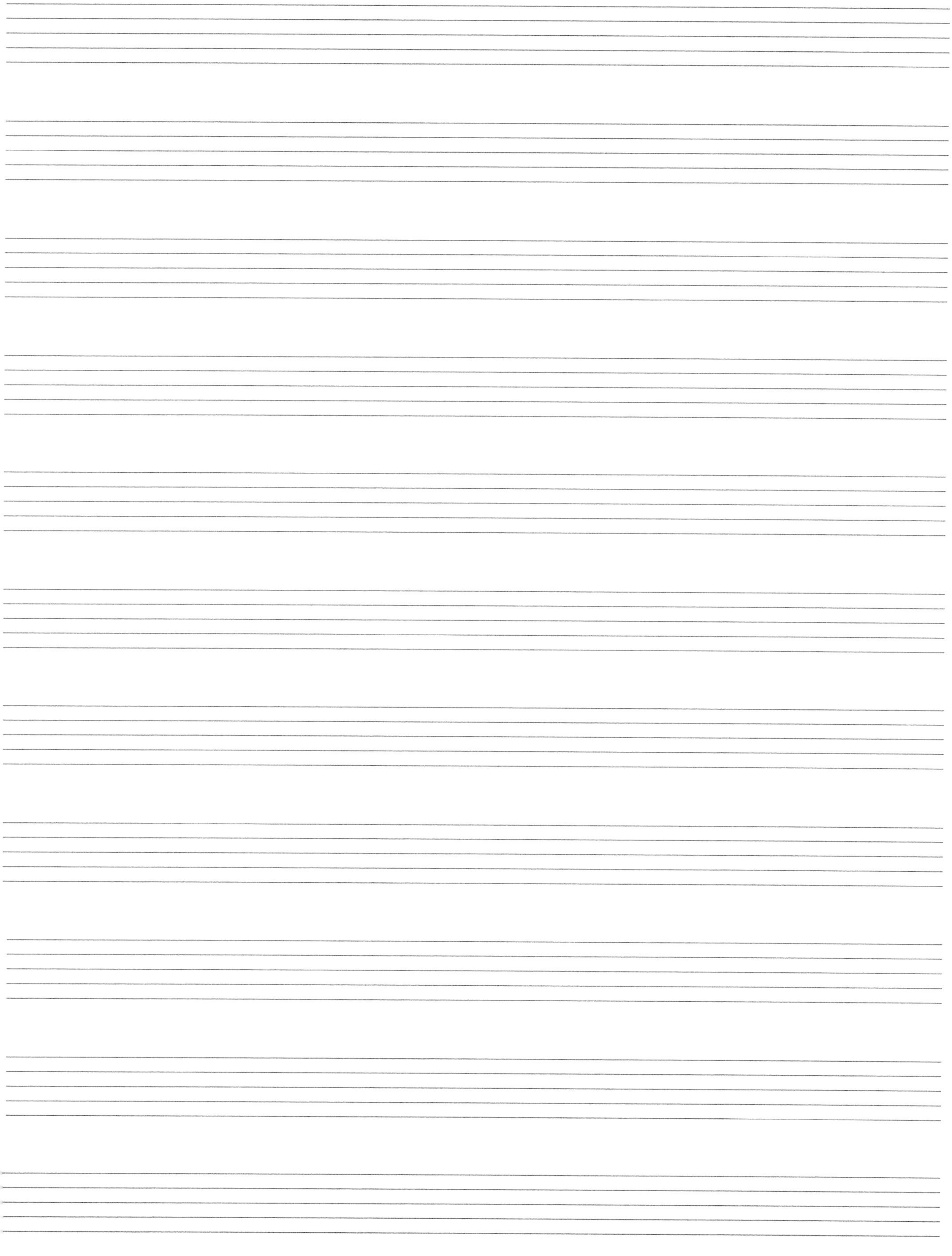

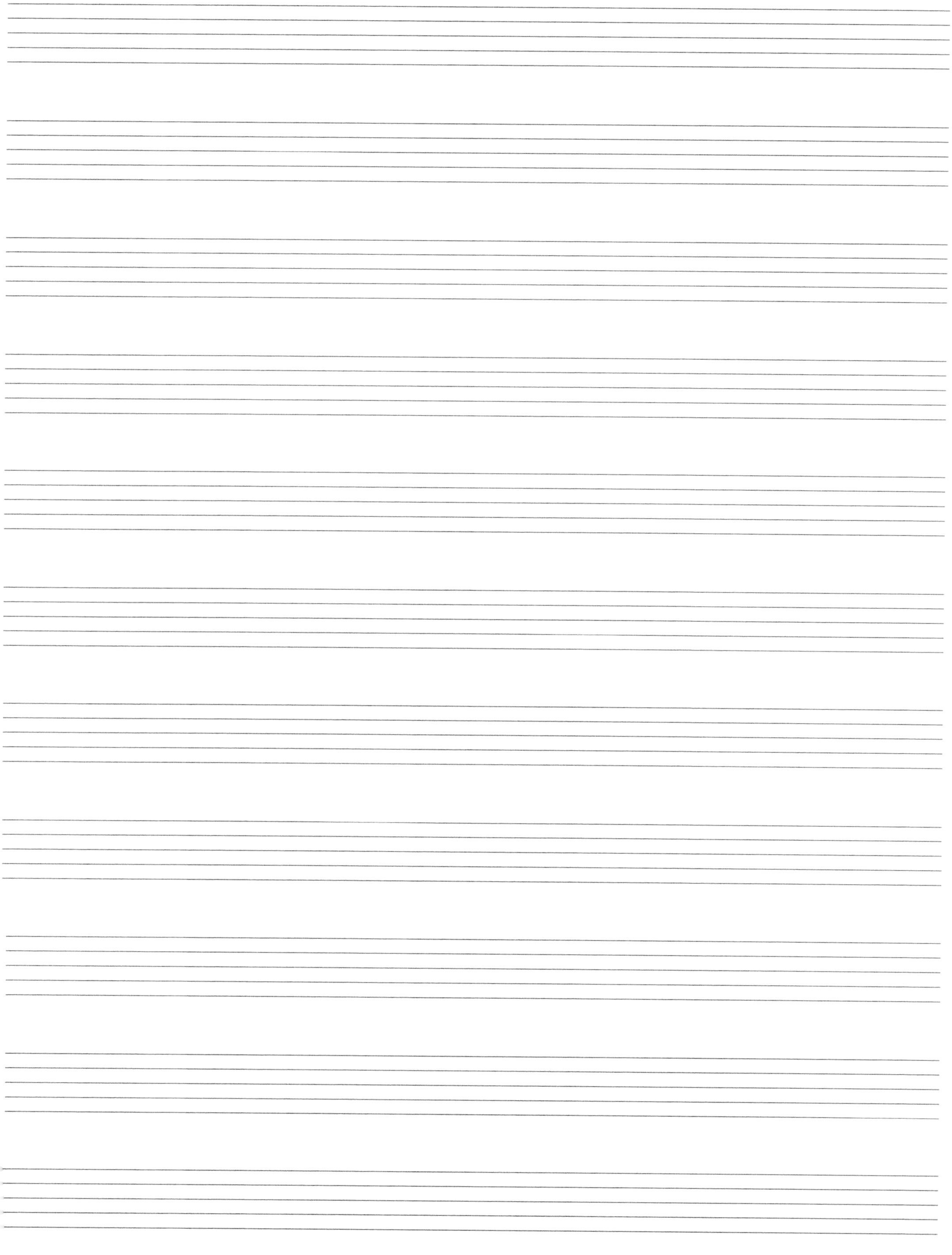

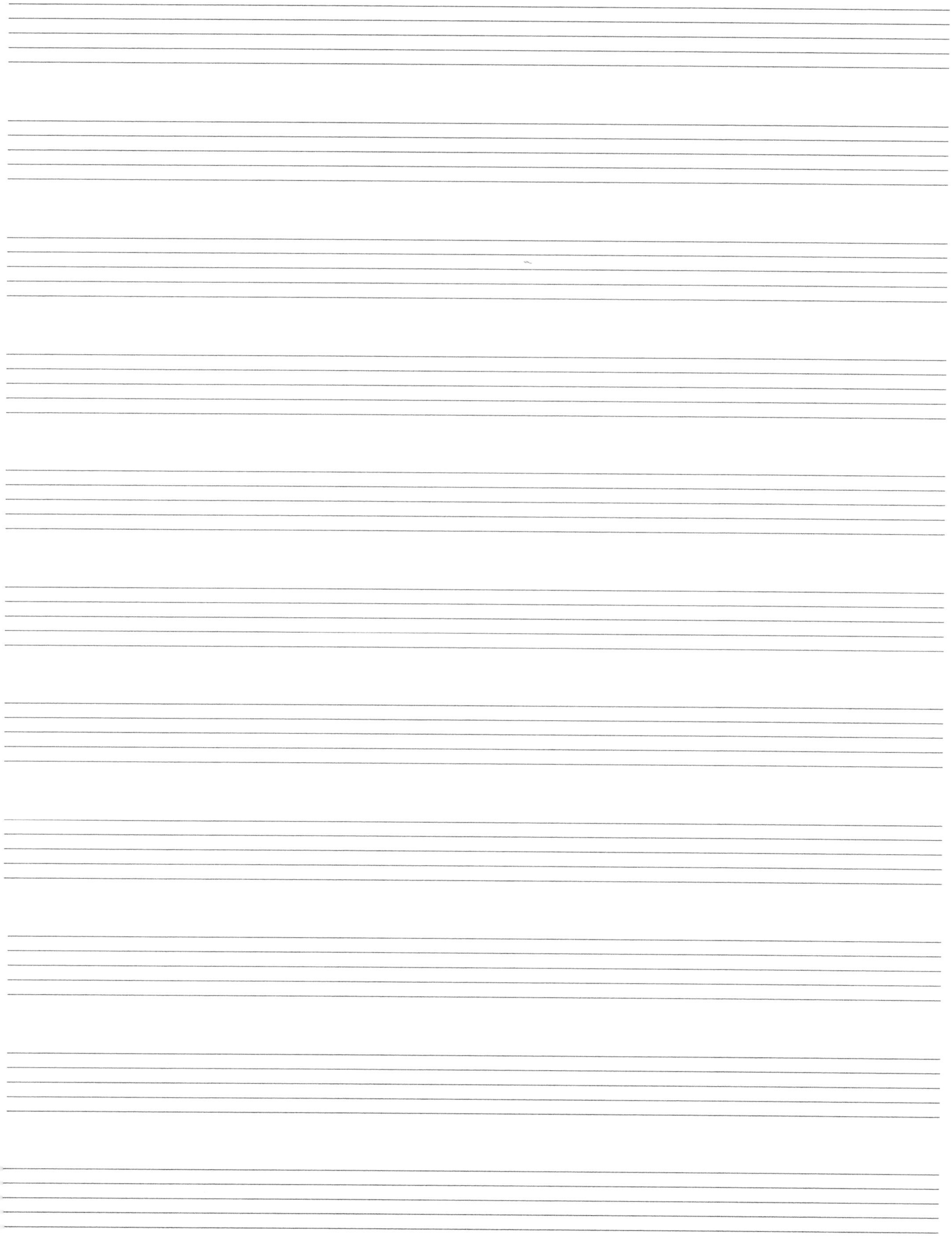

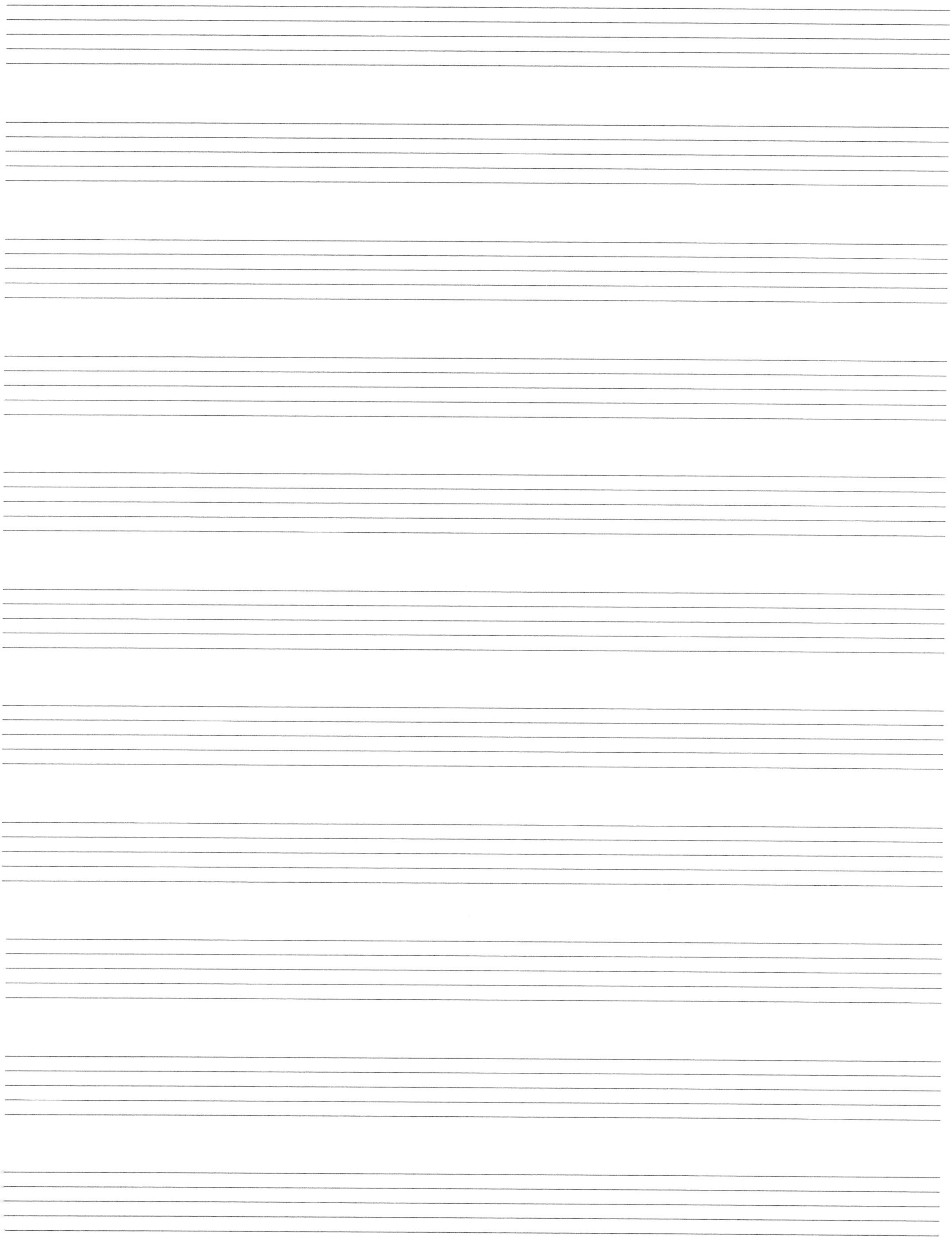

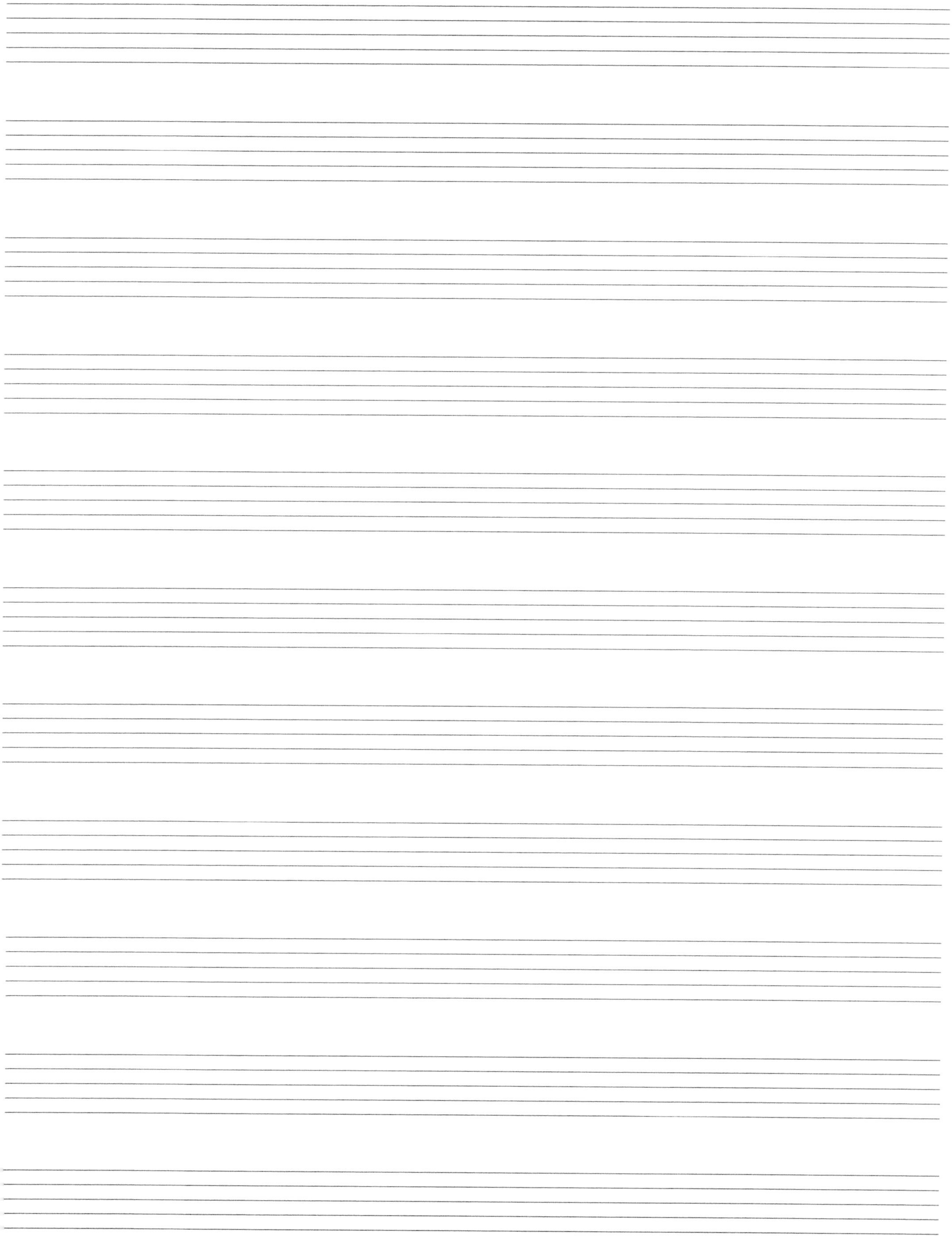

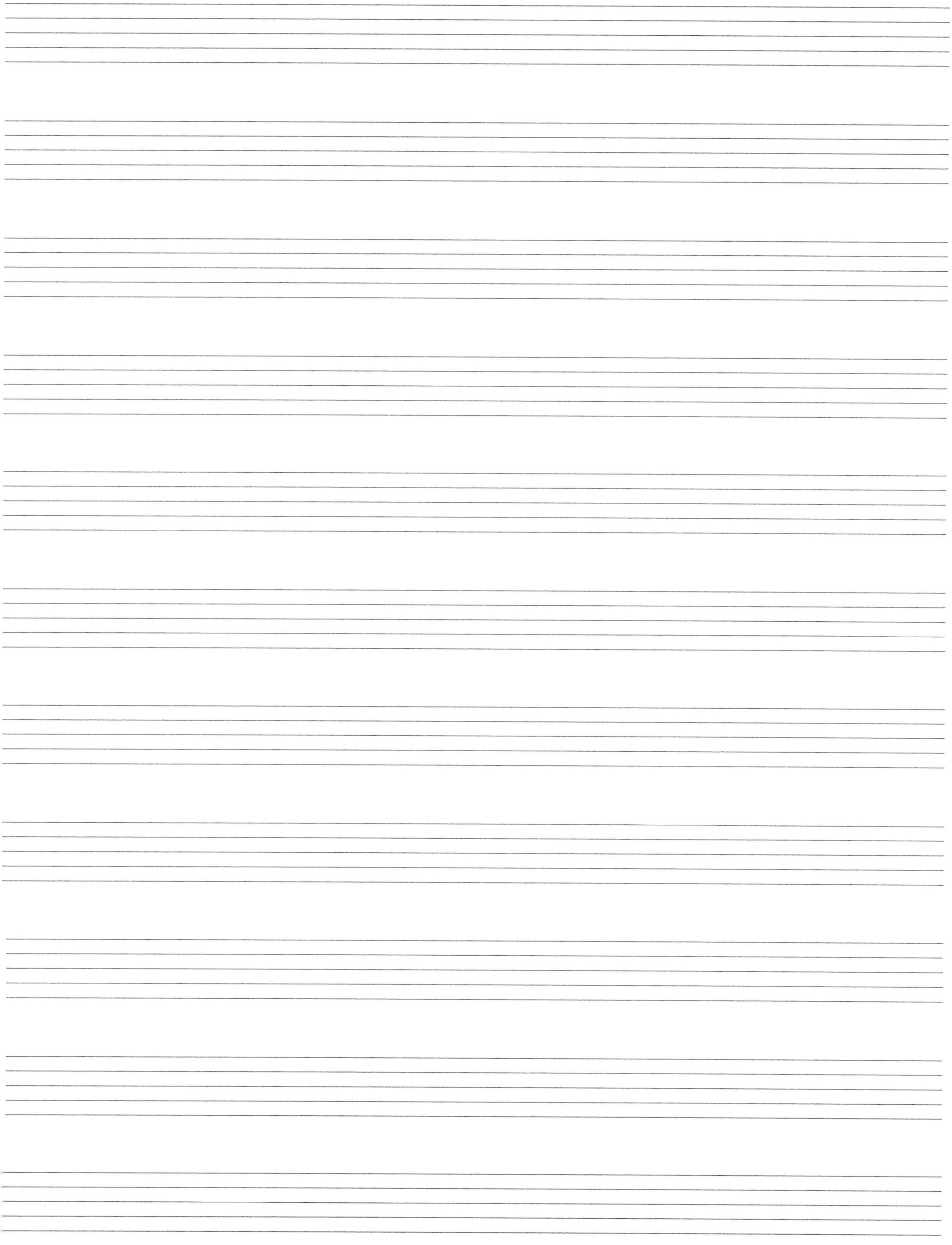

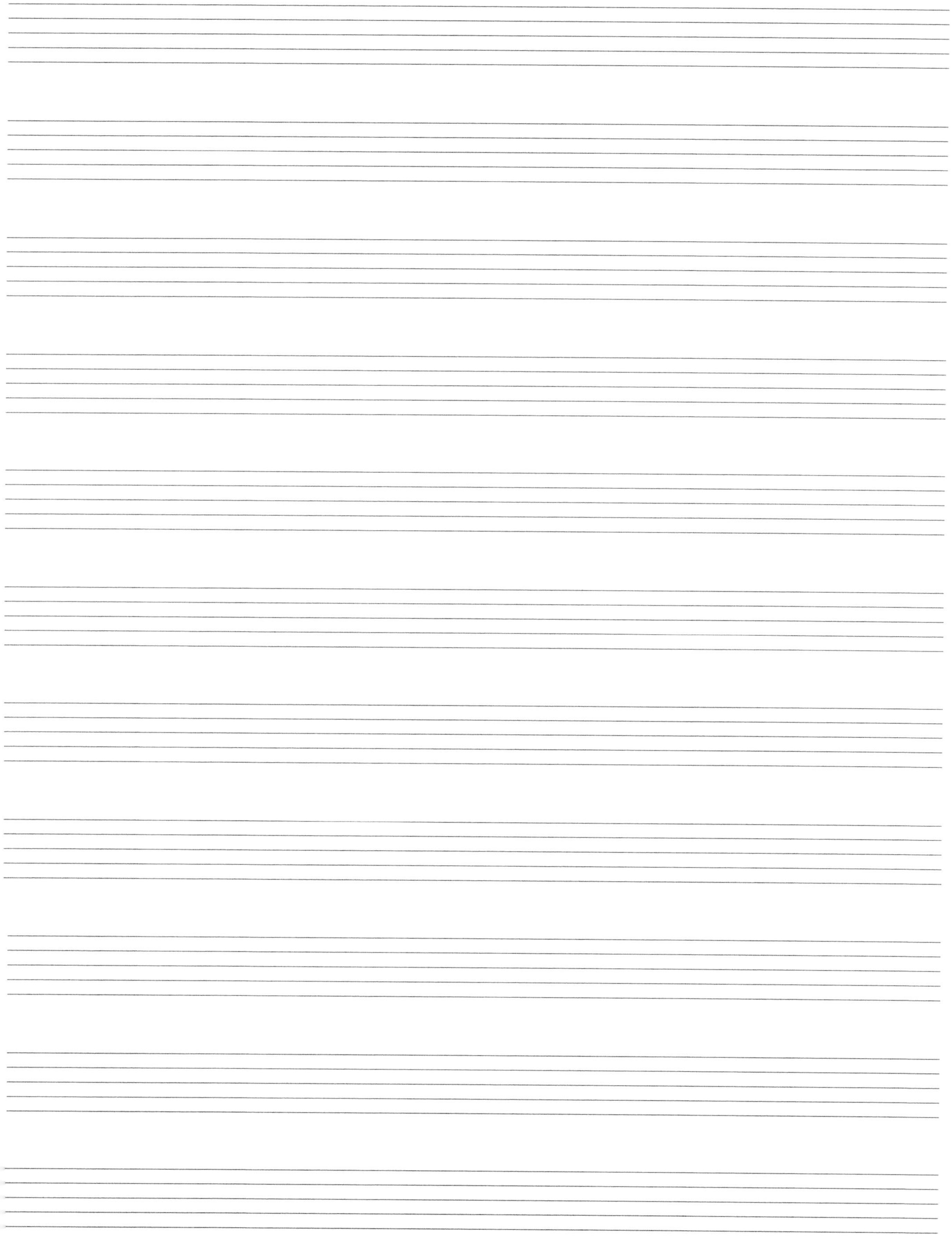

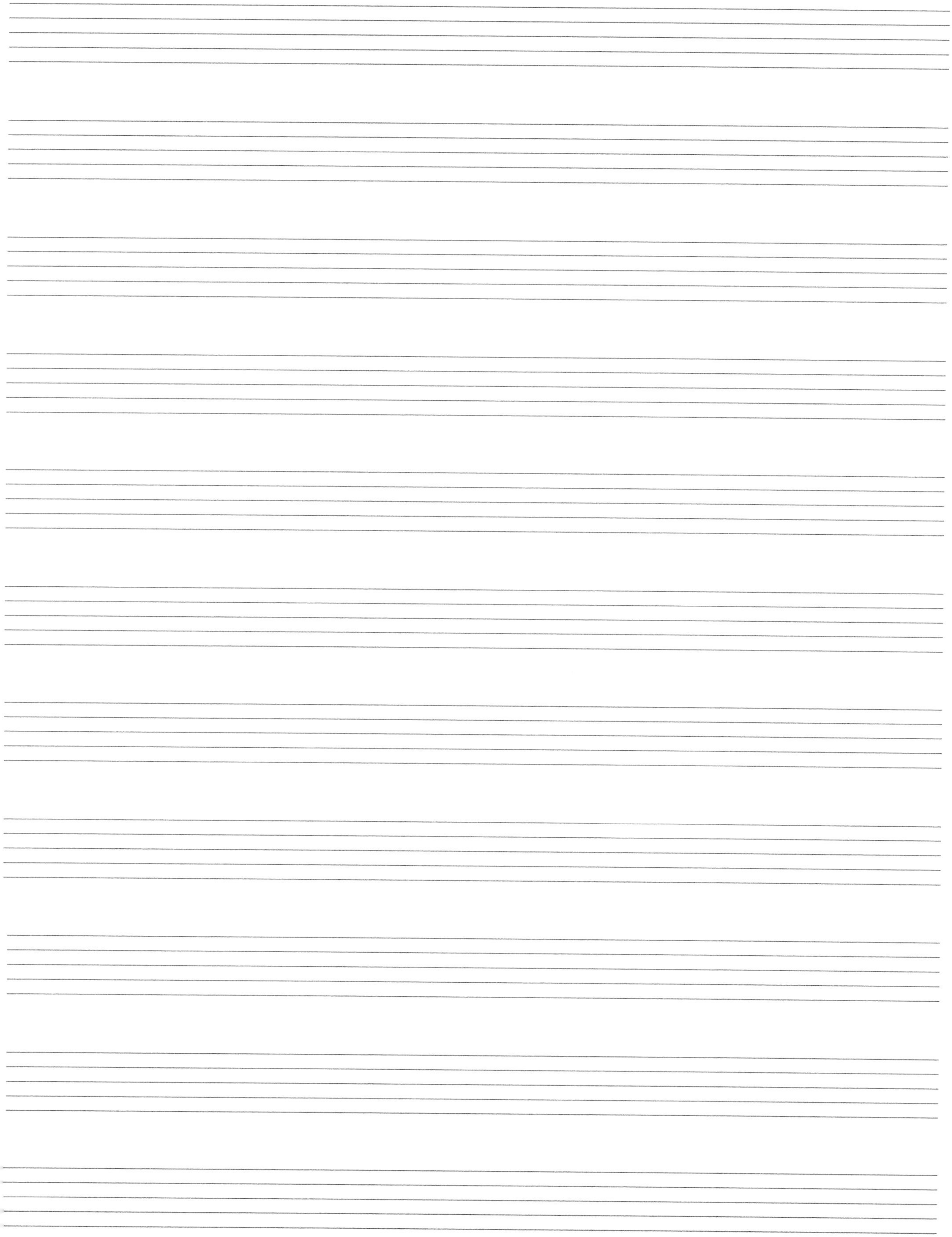

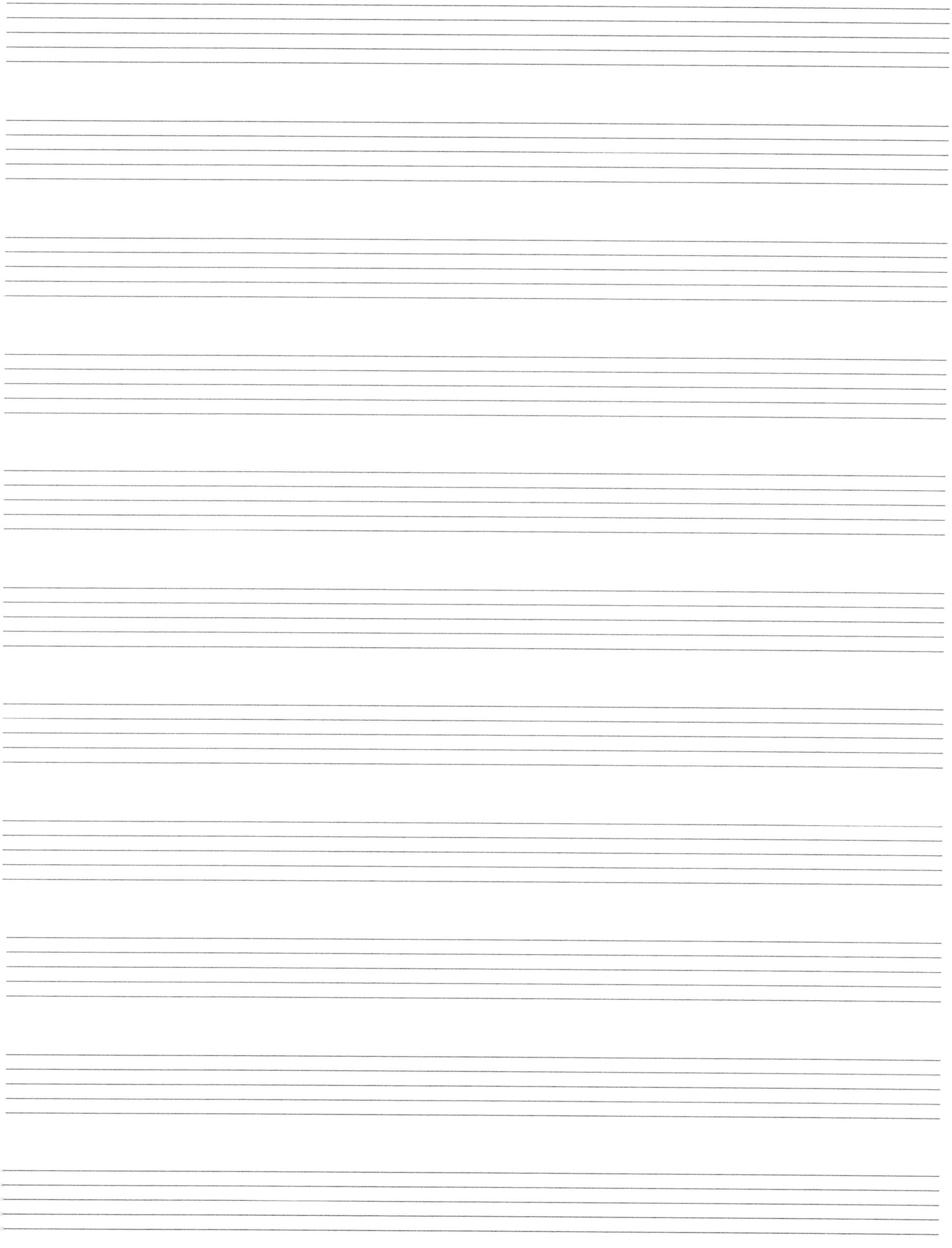

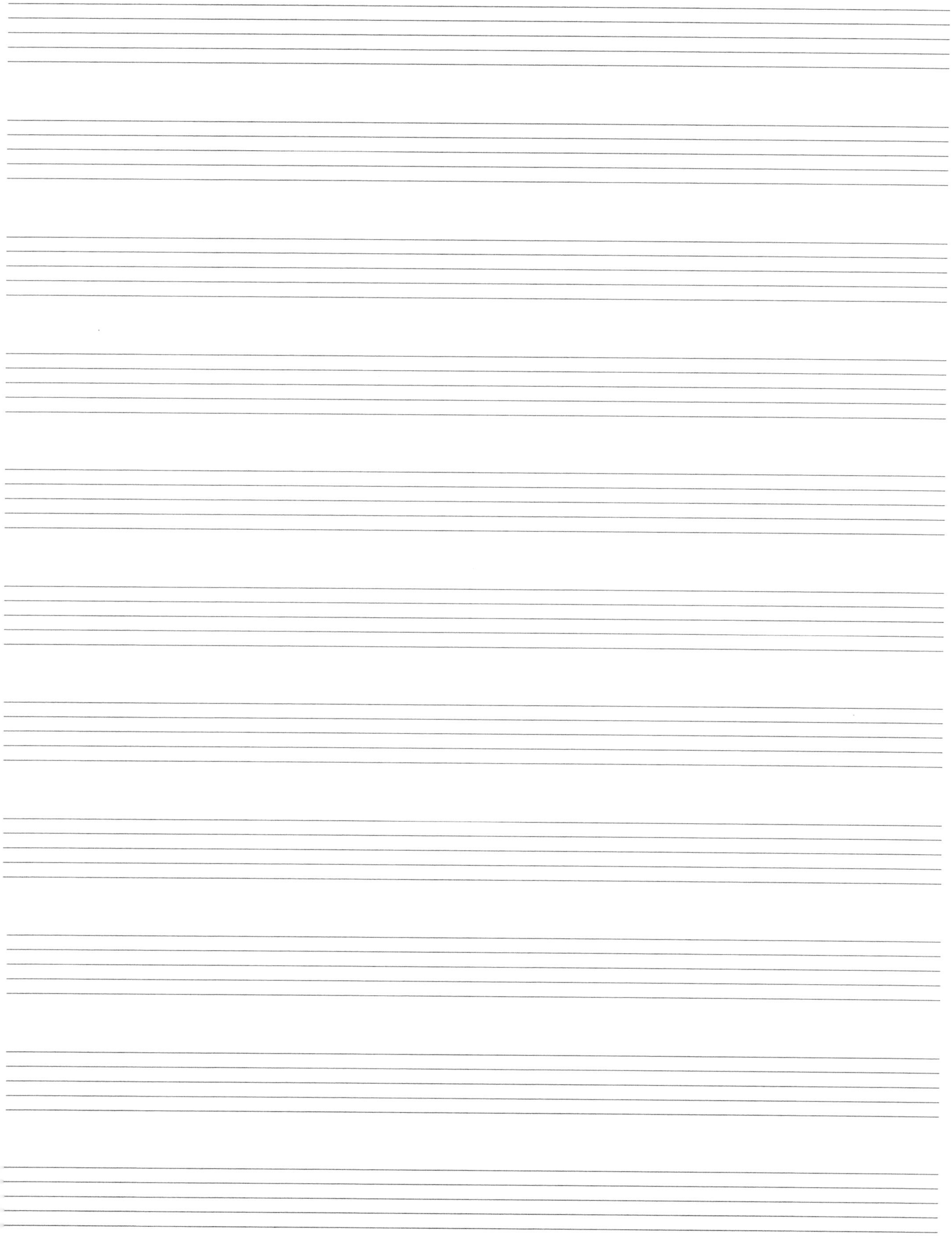

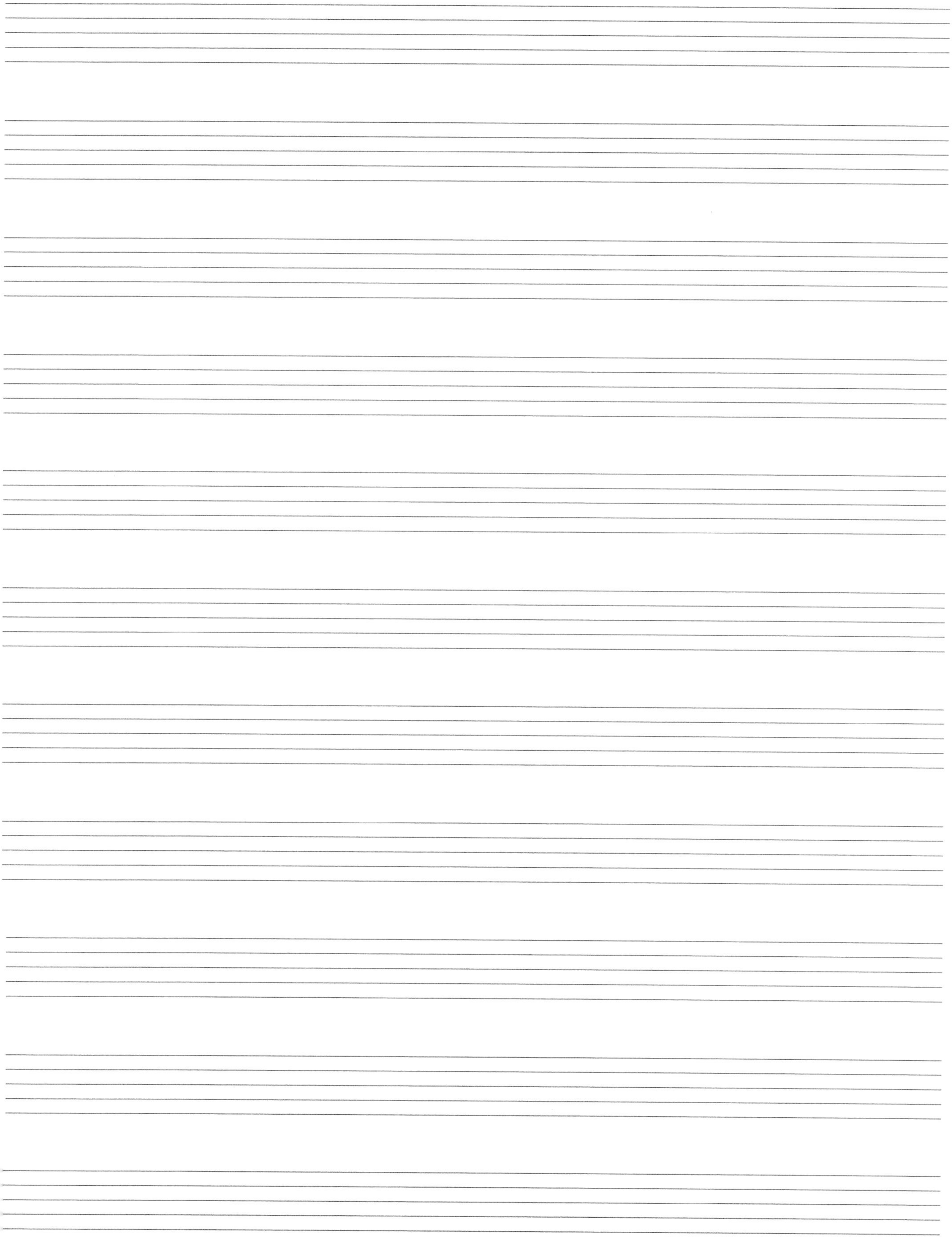

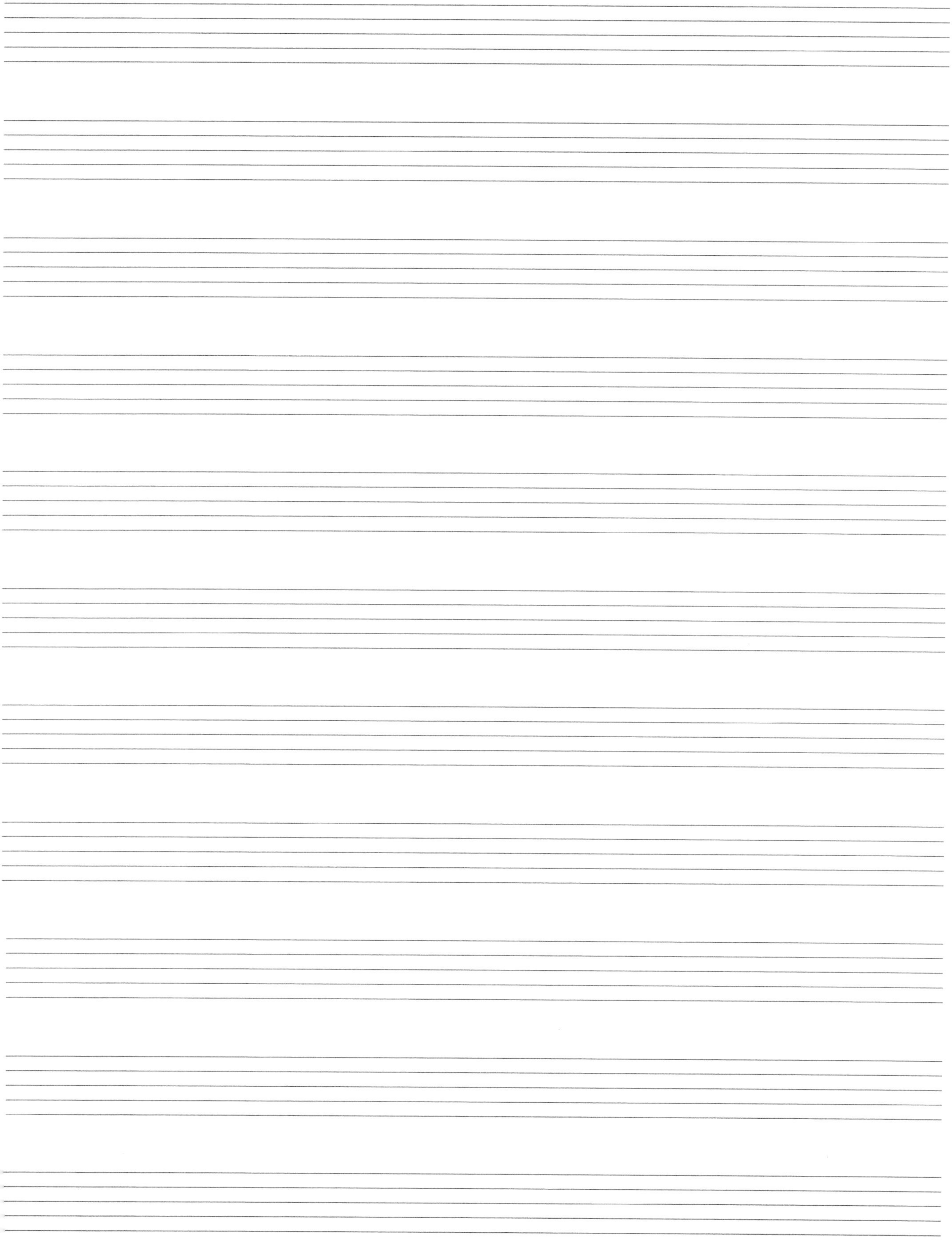

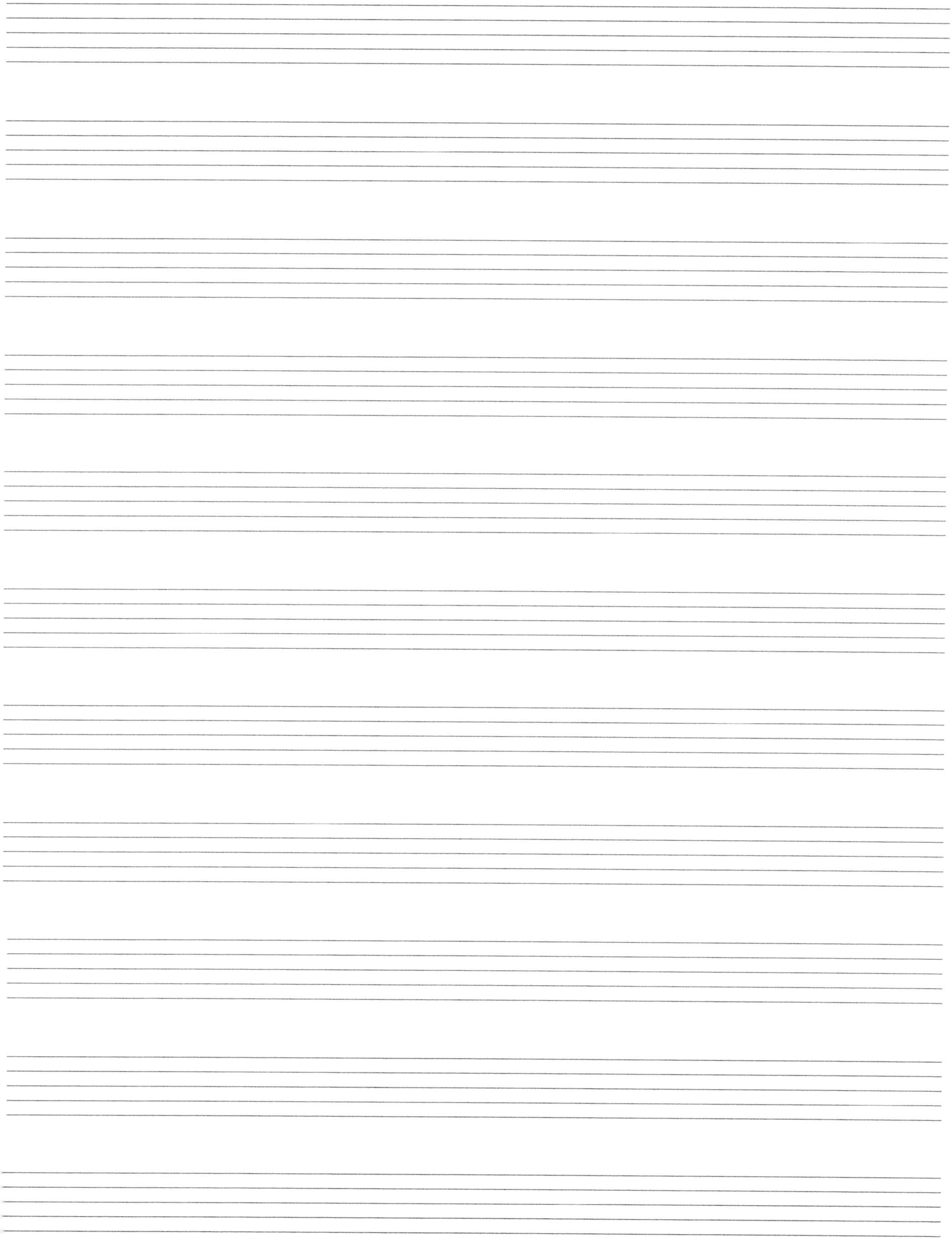

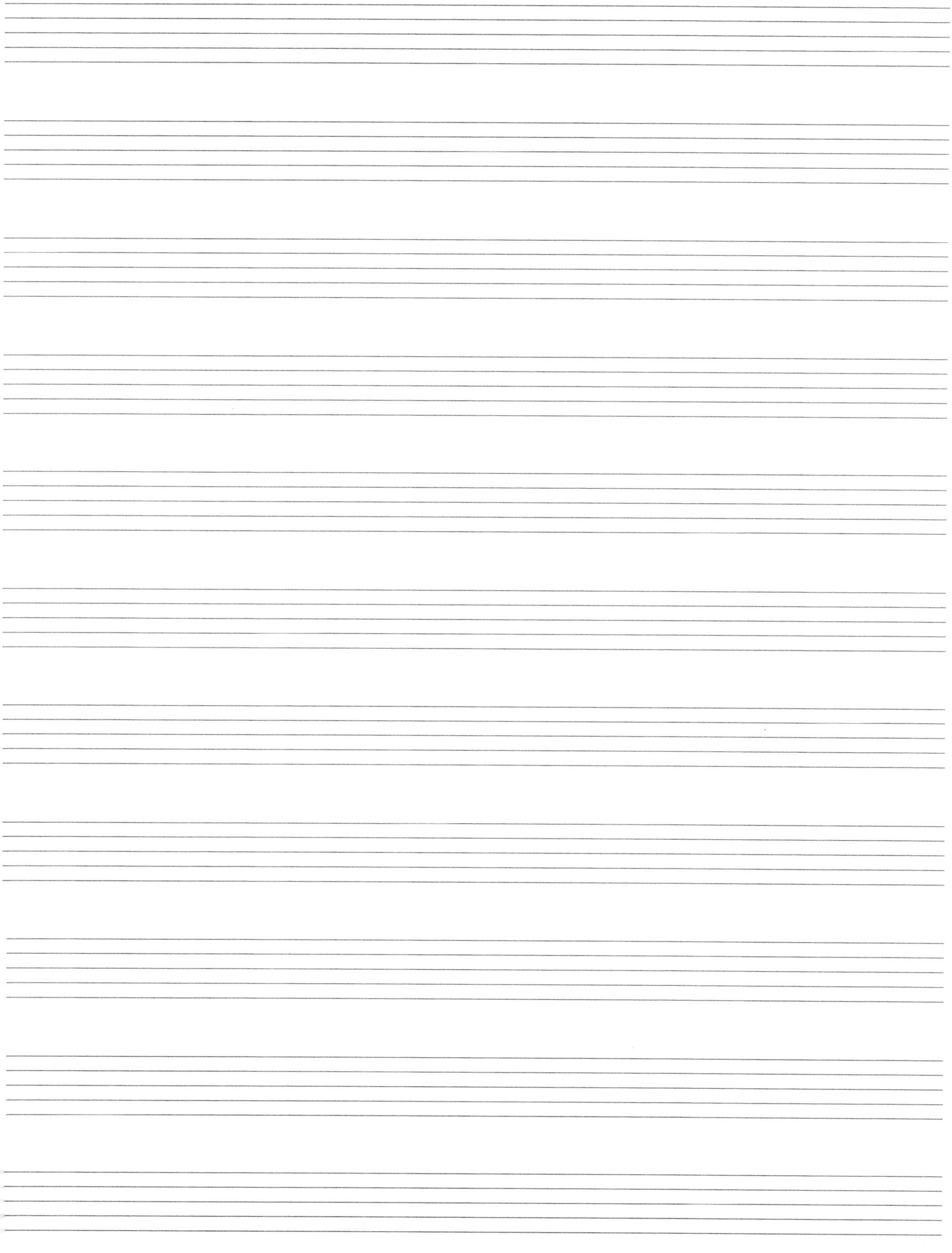

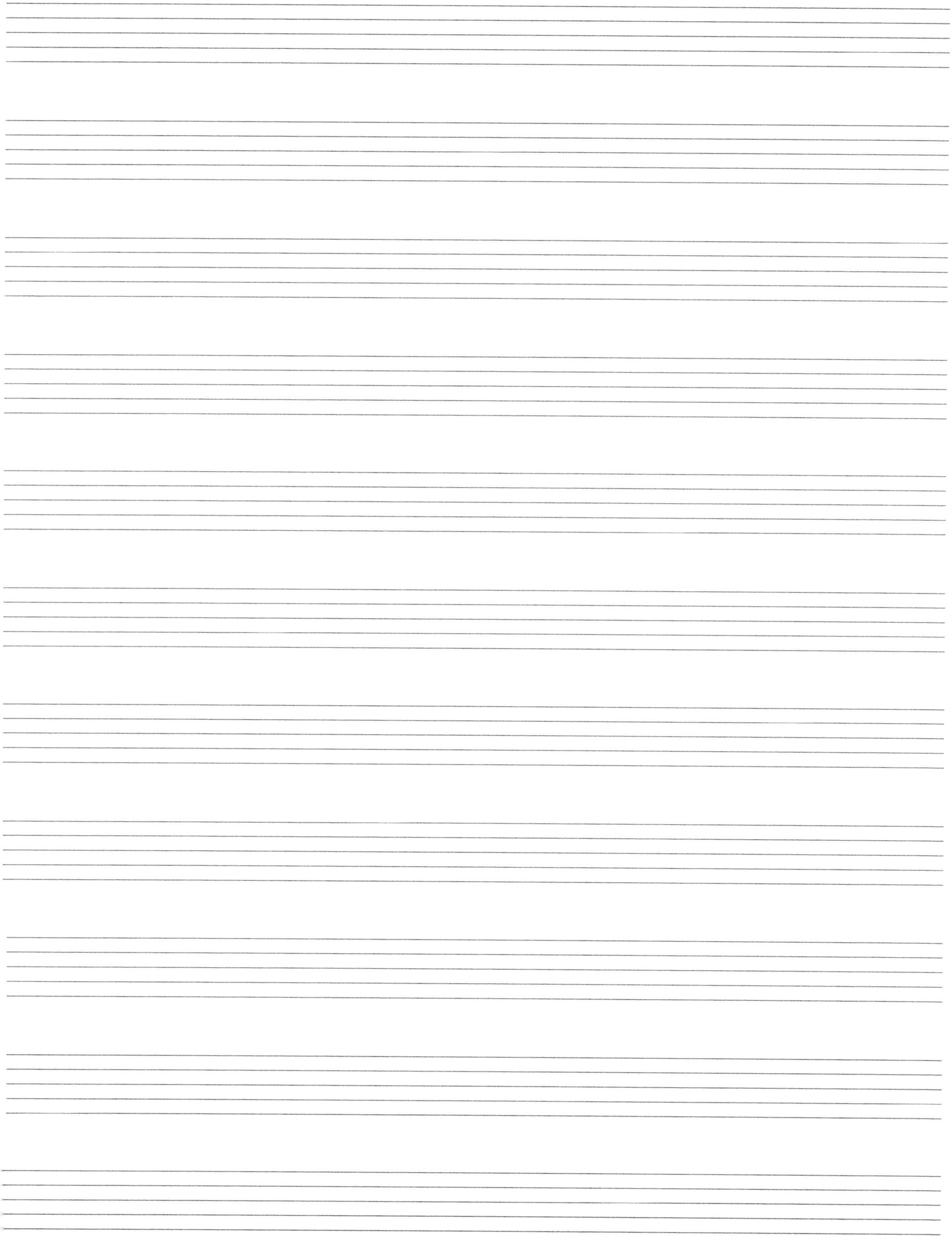

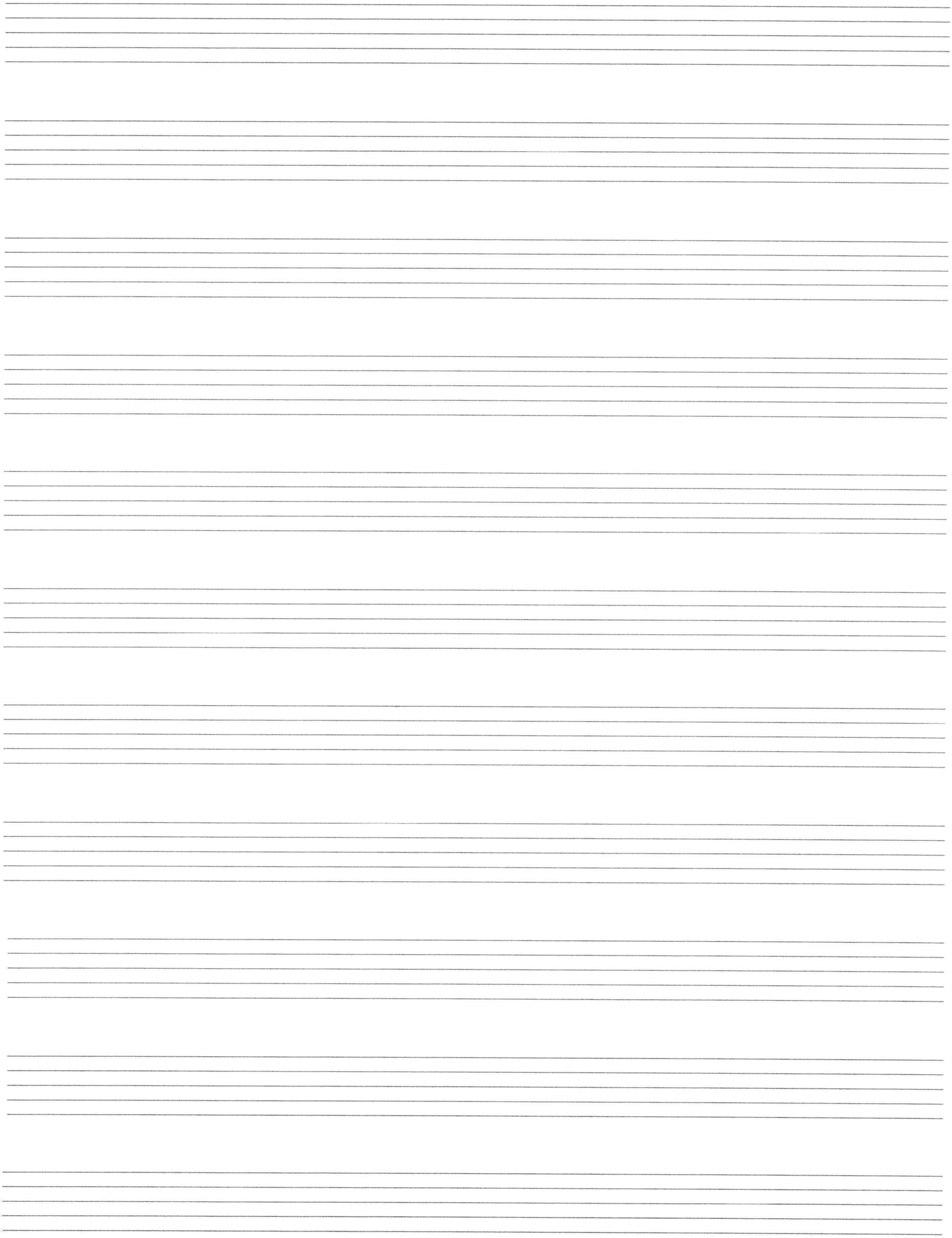

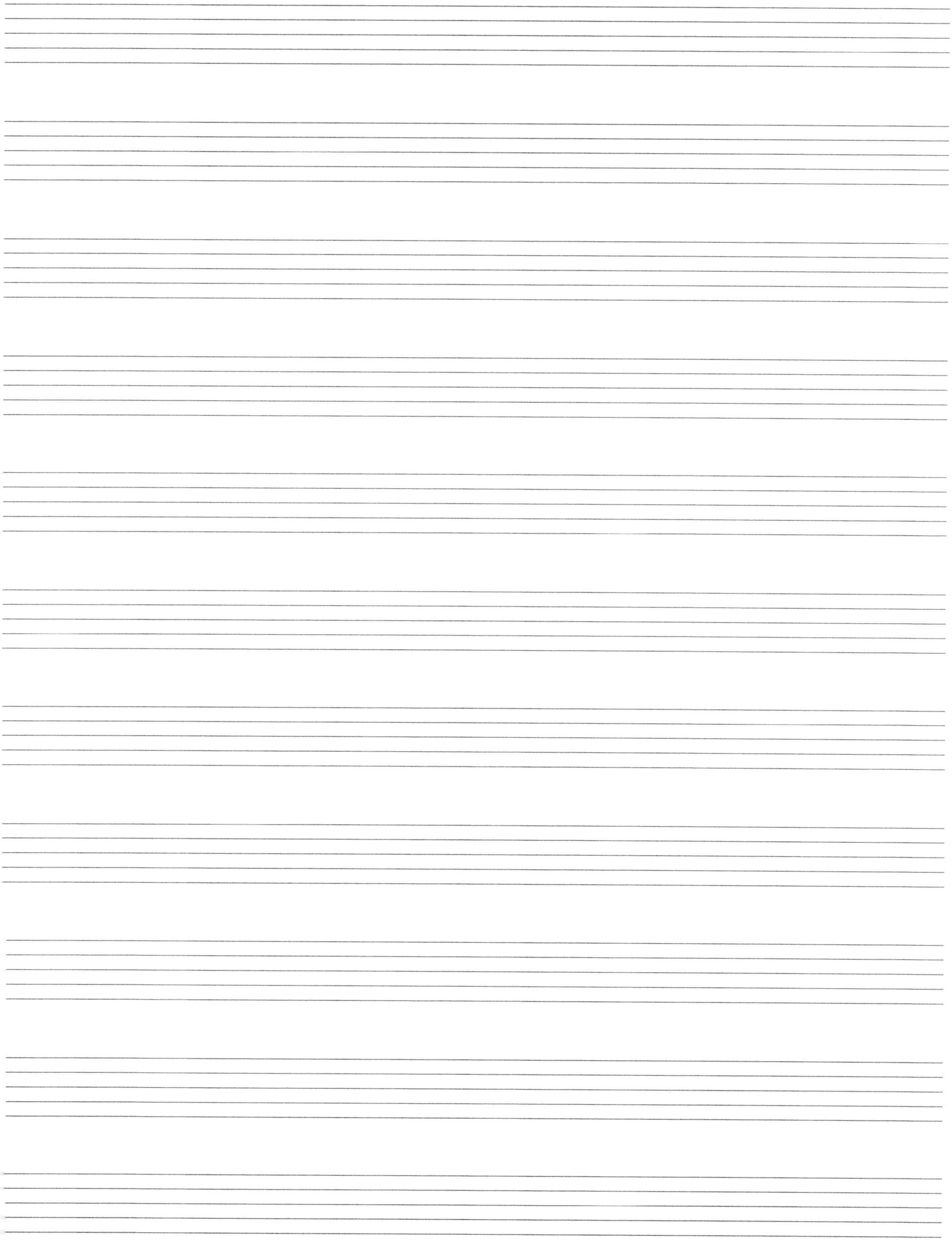

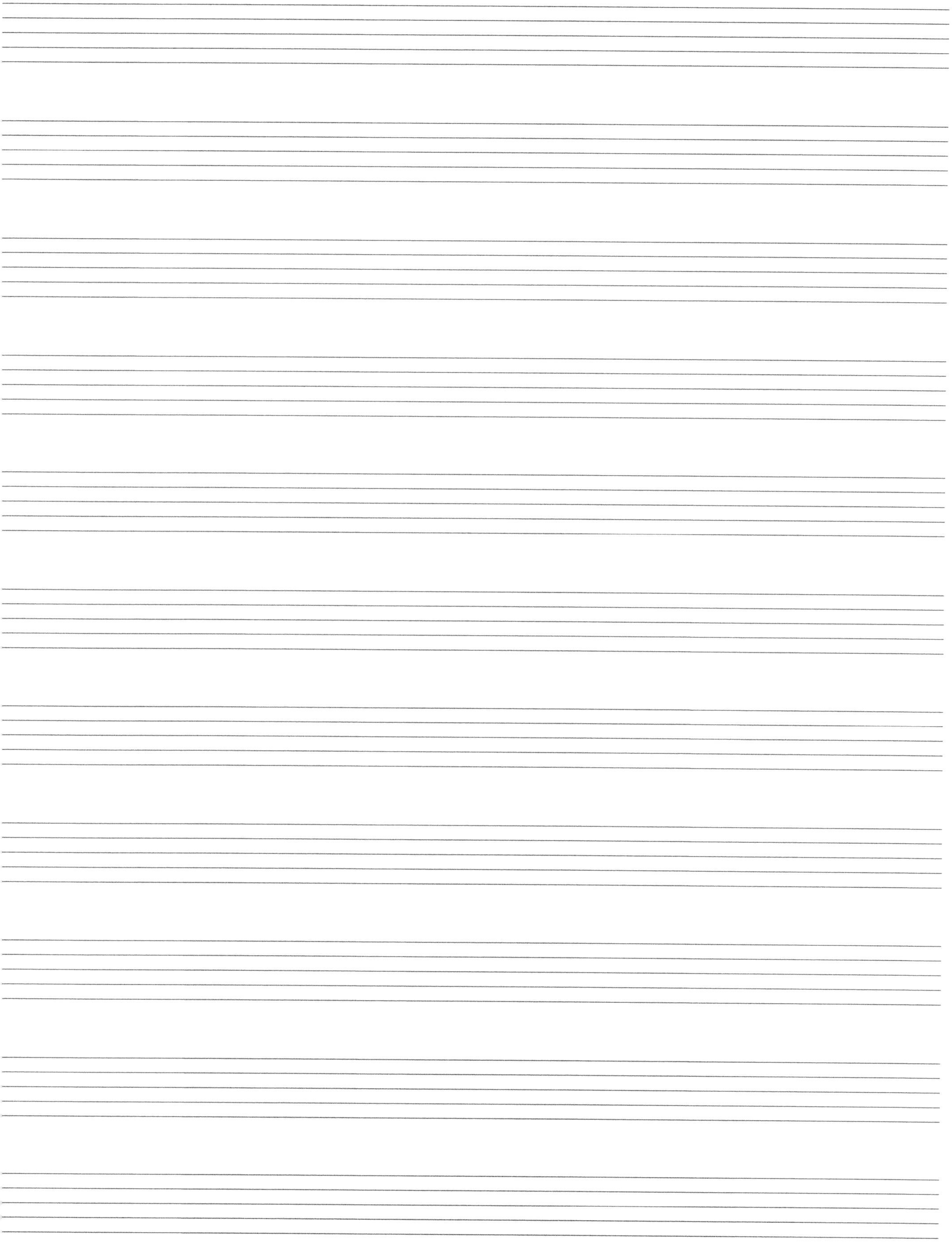

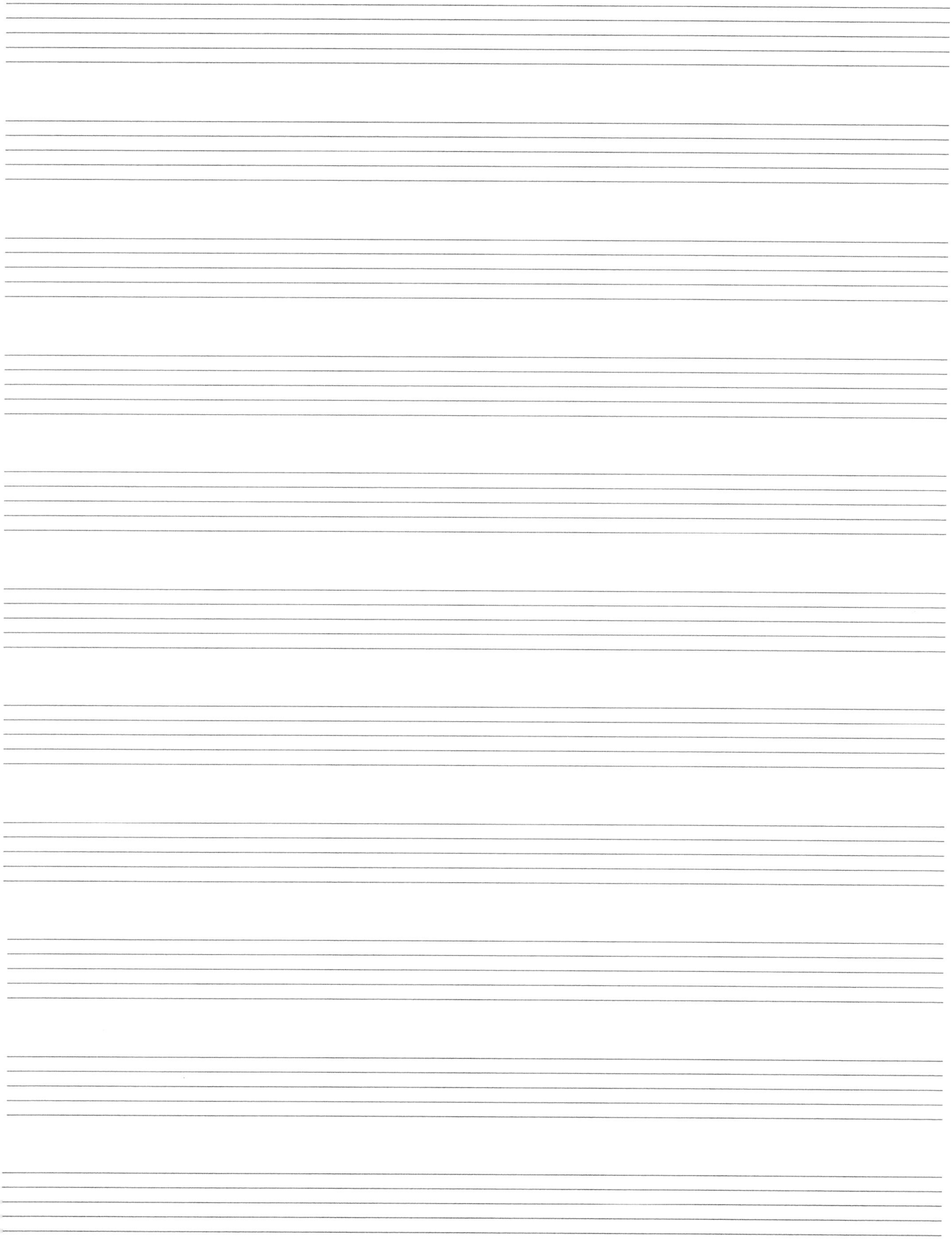

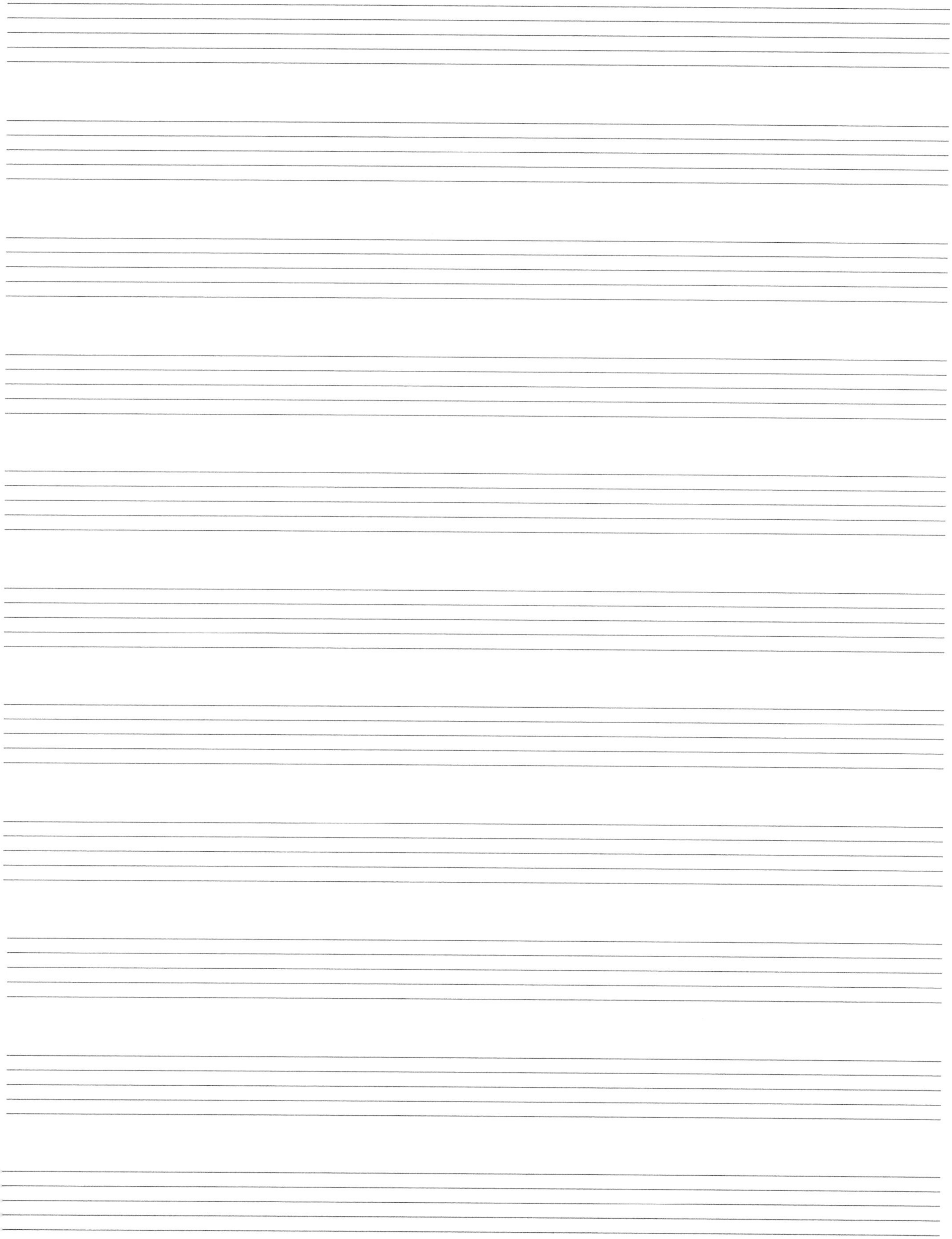

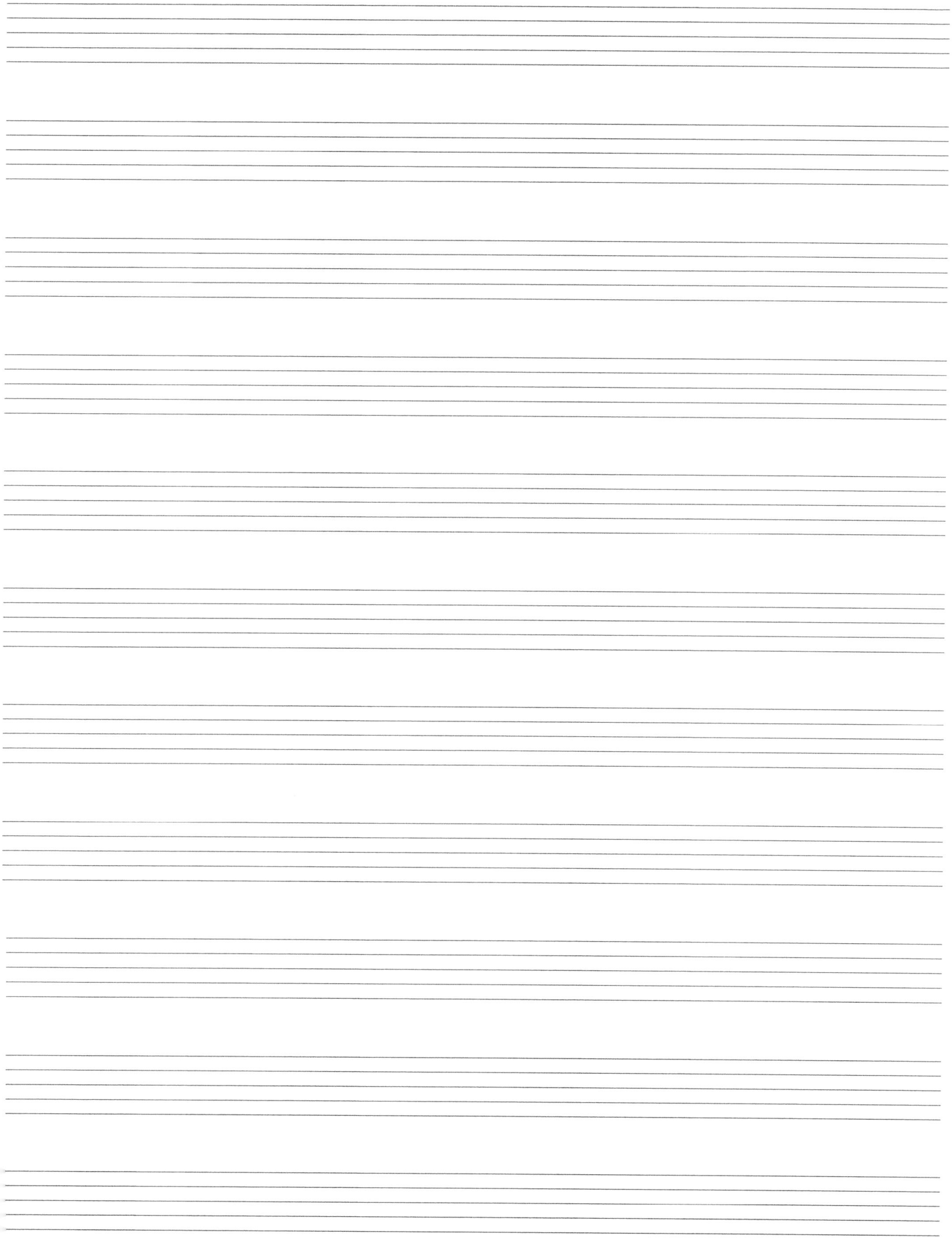

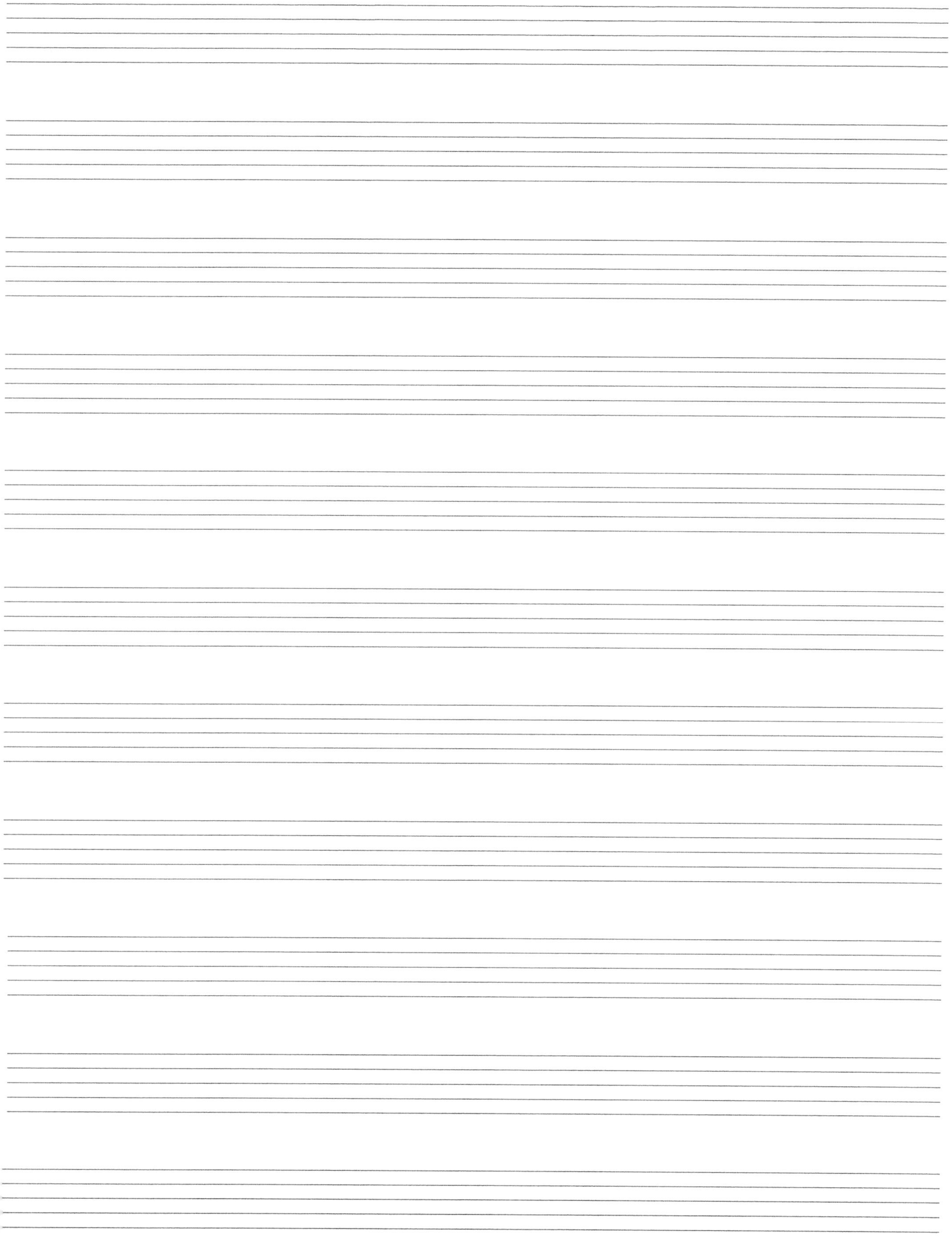

www.ingramcontent.com/pod-product-compliance
Lightning Source LLC
Chambersburg PA
CBHW081548170526
45166CB00009B/2615
* 9 7 8 1 4 7 0 0 7 9 9 4 9 *